THIS JOURNAL
BELONGS TO

SOUL MIRROR

The practice of self-reflection is an active, ongoing, lifelong journey. It's an acknowledgement of your divine connection with your inner being, and an homage to your truest self. This acknowledgement and connection to self is the key to self-healing, spiritual expansion, and advancing the evolution of our collective consciousness.

What is Mirroring?

Mirroring is a form of self-reflection, fast-tracked by seeing your wounds and lessons reflected by the external world—in everyone and everything. Mirroring involves being conscious of yourself from a third-person perspective. Watching your emotions, behaviour, language, actions and energetic exchanges from the point of view of all that resides outside of self.

In practising mirroring, you will become conscious of how a person—their words or actions—the environment, a situation, or anything else external makes you feel internally.

These external encounters will tell you something about yourself through the reflection they offer. Whenever your energy shifts from its happy medium, it will illuminate something that wants your attention to learn, work on or let go of.

When you are in a free-flowing state, this signals harmony and balance and that you are in truth, aligned with loving energy. Anything that tips towards fear is a misalignment or internal 'knot'. This highlighted discomfort is a golden thread of significant information. We need to listen to it.

It's also important to recognise what is yours and what is not yours to heal within the boundaries you create. Sometimes the healing or lesson is not in the situation itself, but in your reaction to it.

Untying and Evolving

When you feel discomfort, allow yourself to move through any emotions that are present and arrive at understanding — this reflection gives you a chance to untie an idle knot that no longer serves you. See this as a beautiful opportunity. By the light of this reflection, acknowledge the knot and then heal it.

As human beings, we all have our unique shadows, emotional traumas, past-life wounds and intergenerational grief to navigate. The practice of mirroring may bring these to the surface to be healed. This can be confronting. But take heart—your soul is ready for change and guidance.

You have everything you need to meet new levels of self-enlightenment and soul expansion.

We have all come to Earth to experience this 3D reality for our spiritual growth. It is an honour to learn and evolve through this experience with others, through all that the earth realm is constantly mirroring back to us, showing us who we are. This is a wondrous gift, bound by the loving grace of our connection with ourselves and each other.

Meeting the World as a Soul Mirror

Through you, divine energy flows. First, from your awareness to your heart, through your body, and then exponentially from your mind into the outer world, creating and merging with the external fabric of life and the collective co-creation—defining our existence on this physical earth plane.

When we use the world as a soul mirror, we are bound to want to make the changes we innately feel and see—because it is you talking to yourself, reflected by the external world.

Journalling

Within the pages of this journal are reflections based on the *Soul Mirror Oracle* that serve as gentle guides, inviting you to embark on a transformative process of self-reflection. With each turn of the page, embark on an exploration that illuminates your true essence and brings power and awareness back to yourself.

As you truthfully respond to each reflection, you engage in a powerful dialogue with your soul, unearthing profound insights and nurturing a deeper understanding of self. It becomes a vessel for our thoughts, dreams and desires, encapsulating the journey of our growth, self-expression and ultimate creation.

We are at a pivotal time in our conscious evolution. There is so much unfolding and so much more to come. We all need to take responsibility for growing the healthiest, most honest, and highest versions of ourselves. Doing this will elevate our outer-world experiences as co-creators of life, and the loving and limitless frequency we innately are.

What old perceptions do I need to outgrow to evolve and accept my unveiled, radiant self? Can I let go and be truly free, truly me?

Am I staying true to my core values and inner truth in my daily life? How can I ensure my thoughts and actions reflect the desires of my heart, body and soul?

*How can I cultivate a deeper awareness of the blessings
and gifts in each moment, and honour them?*

What delightful fruits in my life would I like to see?
And how can I fully celebrate their blossoming?

How can I find the comfort and fulfilment I seek from within, rather than relying on external sources?

*How does nurturing my inner seed help
me to co-create a loving and limitless frequency
in my life and our combined 3D reality?*

How can I tap into my creativity and bring my unique visions to life? What steps can I take to create my reality and a world that aligns with my desires and aspirations?

How can I effectively communicate my needs and desires to others, and freely express myself in a way that feels authentic and true to who I am?

What activities bring me back to a state of childlike wonder and excitement? How can I give myself permission to follow my curiosity, even if I don't know where it will lead?

How can I be open to the evolution that is occurring and embrace the changes that come with it? What is the lesson that I need to learn about surrendering to change?

How can I cultivate a sense of gratitude and appreciation for the experiences and opportunities available to me right now?

What are the illusionary limitations that I am ready to push and expand beyond? How can I tap into the infinitely supplied energy of love to fuel my creative force?

*What steps can I take to let go of any hindrances
and freely share my joy with myself and others?*

What actions can I take to cultivate a sense of gratitude and appreciation?
How can I approach all situations with a loving and compassionate mindset?

How can I trust and believe in the guidance and support I receive from the Universe as I navigate through my growth and evolution?

In what ways do external noise and distractions dilute my connection with my intuition? How does following my intuition lead to clarity and divine guidance?

Can I open up to access the deep-rooted knowledge within me from all layers of my being — past, present and future?

*Can I choose to approach my interactions
with love and understanding?*

How can I cultivate a sense of curiosity and openness to new perspectives, and actively seek out opportunities for self-discovery and growth?

Can I embrace life lessons and see them as opportunities for growth and self-development? What can I do to channel the free-flowing energy of my lessons into the world, and support others in their own journeys of growth and evolution?

How can I cultivate a strong and stable centre, and rely on my own resources to navigate challenges and find calm and tranquillity?

How can I use my power to shift my perspective to create a positive and fulfilling future for myself and those around me?

What gateways and portals can I open to invite the magic within?

How can I tap into my limitless power and unleash my potential? What steps can I take to inspire and awaken others to their own infinite potential?

How will I stand in my power and reclaim what I have forgotten or lost through lack of belief?

How can I cultivate a mindset of gratitude and recognise the blessings and gifts in my life, even in the face of challenges?

How do I take responsibility for my thoughts, emotions and actions in shaping the reality I co-create?

What steps can I take to empower myself and heal my sense of security from within?

*How can I initiate new gateways and portals within myself
to express the magic within the physical realm?*

What self-imposed cage of seeking do I need to release in order to see my true self?
How can I trust and believe that I have everything I need within me?